55 FUI ____

FACTS

ABOUT

DINOSAURS

By

The Dino Detective

Introduction

Dinosaurs were probably the most amazing creatures to have ever walked on the surface of our planet Earth! They came in all kinds of shapes and sizes. Some dinosaurs grew to be larger than a school bus, while others were only the size of a cat. Some had huge heads with a mouth full of giant teeth for eating the flesh of other dinosaurs, while others sported very long necks for eating the leaves from the tops of the tallest trees. Other dinosaurs were covered in a bony type of natural armour for protection. Finally you may be amazed to learn that some dinosaurs may have been covered with feathers!

In book 4 of the Dinosaur Books for Kids series called "55 Funky Facts about Dinosaurs", you will learn just how truly amazing the dinosaurs really were by discovering the answers to question such as:

How Many Different Kinds Of Dinosaurs Where There?

Which Dinosaurs Have Been Found In The Most Places In The World?

Which Dinosaur Had The Largest Teeth?

Which Was The Smallest Of The Dinosaurs?

Which Dinosaur Could Run The Fastest?

And 50 more funky facts about dinosaurs, including some terrific pictures of what we believe these dinosaurs may have actually looked like based on recent scientific research and fossil remains. So let's get started on our journey to discover "*55 Funky Facts about Dinosaurs*"!

When did the first dinosaurs appear?

Funky Dino Fact 1:

Some 225 million years ago, dinosaurs began to evolve from crocodile like creatures. Two of the earliest dinosaurs discovered lived in parts of what we now call the continent of South America at the beginning of the late Triassic period. They were called *Herrerasaurus* (say "He-ray-raar-sore-uss") and *Staurikosaurus* (say "Store-ick-owe-sore-uss"). Both of these early dinosaurs were meat-eaters.

Herrerasaurus   *Staurikosaurus*

When did the dinosaurs disappear and why?

Funky Dino Fact 2:
There are a number of theories or suggestions as to why the dinosaurs disappeared. The most widely accepted theory today states that about 65 million years ago a huge asteroid from space crashed into the Earth.

The massive impact of this object hitting the Earth killed many dinosaurs after the explosion, but the worst was yet to come. Enormous amounts of dust and other particles such as soot and ash were thrown into our atmosphere blocking out much of the sunlight for many months which causes the temperature around the world to suddenly drop to the point that many of the plants needed to feed the plant-eating dinosaurs died. Without food the plant-eaters began to die and this also spelled the end for the meat-eaters who depended on the plant-eating dinosaurs for their food.

How do we name the dinosaurs?

Funky Dino Fact 3:
Each and every dinosaur name is made up of two parts. The first is called the genus and begins with a capital letter. The second part is the species name and it does not begin with a capital letter. Both names are generally typed in italic lettering. Similar species or types of dinosaurs are generally grouped together in the same genus. For example, you may have already seen the dinosaur name *Tyrannosaurus* (say "Tie-ran-owe-sore-uss") *rex* which was a large meat-eating dinosaur. Often people simply refer to such dinosaurs by the genus name of *Tyrannosaurus*.

Tyrannosaurus rex

How many different kinds of dinosaurs were there?

Funky Dino Fact 4:
Scientist estimate the numbers of different kinds of dinosaurs to be somewhere between 900 and 1,200. Yet at this time many experts feel that we have only discovered about 25% of all the different types of dinosaurs that had ever lived.

Lots of dinosaurs

Which areas of the world had the most kinds of dinosaurs?

Funky Dino Fact 5:
Sedimentary rock formations formed in the Triassic, Jurassic and Cretaceous Periods, hundreds of millions of ago, in parts of the western United States and Canada hold claim to the largest numbers of different kinds of dinosaurs at this time. Fossil records from these sedimentary rock beds show a wide range of dinosaurs of all types existed in these areas including meat-eaters such as *Allosaurus* (say "Al-owe-sore-uss"), long-necked plant-eaters such as *Brachiosaurus* (say" Brach-ee-owe-sore-uss"), armoured dinosaurs like *Stegosaurus* (say "Steg-owe-sore-uss") and the horned dinosaurs including *Triceratops* (say "Try-serra-tops").

Allosaurus

Brachiosaurus

Stegosaurus

Triceratops

Which dinosaurs have been found in the most places in the world?

Funky Dino Fact 6:

At this time, the *Iguanodon* (say "Ig-wan-oh-don") holds this title. *Iguanodon* fossils have been found in many parts of the world including the United States, Europe and even in parts of Asia (Mongolia). Other dinosaurs that have been found in many parts of the world include the *Brachiosaurus*, found in parts of the North America (Colorado) and Africa (Tanzania), and *Psittacosaurus* (say "Sit-ah-coe-sore-uss"), which roamed parts large areas of Asia (China, Mongolia and Siberia).

Iguanodon

Brachiosaurus

Psittacosaurus

Which dinosaurs lived the farthest south?

Funky Dino Fact 7:
In parts of southeastern Australia, scientists have discovered a number of dinosaur types including the armoured *Minmi* (say "Min-mee"). Recently dinosaur fossils that have yet to be identified have been discovered in Antarctica proving that hundreds of millions of years ago, this huge frozen landmass actually had a warm, tropical climate.

Minmi

Which dinosaurs lived the farthest north?

Funky Dino Fact 8:
Remains of a type of dinosaur called a "duckbill" (due to having a snout like a duck) have been found in what we know as the area of Alaska. Dinosaur foot prints have been discovered even further north, up in the Arctic on the island of Spitzbergen.

Alaska dinosaur footprint

What was the tallest dinosaur?

Funky Dino Fact 9:
Currently this title is held by a huge plant-eating dinosaur with the name *Ultrasauros* (say "Ull-trah-sore-oss"). It had a very long neck and when stretched out, its head could be raised to a height of 55 feet (16.8 meters) above the ground to allow for tree top dining.

Ultrasauros

Which dinosaur was the heaviest?

Funky Dino Fact 10:
Many experts give this award to *Ultrasauros*, (say "Ull-trah-sore-oss"), who was believed to have weighed as much as 100 tons or 200,000 pounds (91 metric tonnes or 91,000 kilograms).

Ultrasauros

Which dinosaur was the longest?

Funky Dino Fact 11:
A long-necked plant-eating dinosaur with the name of *Seismosaurus* (say "Size-mow-sore-uss") currently hold this award. From the skeletal remains discovered, scientists believe that a fully grown *Seismosaurus* may have reached more than 130 feet (39.6 meters) long.

Seismosaurus

Which dinosaur had the most body armour?

Funky Dino Fact 12:
Many dinosaurs had some type of boney armour for protection, but the title of most heavily armoured goes to the 25 foot (7.6 meter) long, *Ankylosaurus* (say "Ann-kye-low-sore-uss"). It even had boney armour covering its eyelids!

Ankylosaurus

Which dinosaur had the biggest head?

Funky Dino Fact 13:
The group of dinosaurs known as "horned dinosaurs" easily recognized by not only by horns on their head, but also big frills covering their necks, are generally accepted as having the largest heads or skulls. One type, called *Torosaurus* (say "Torr-owe-sore-uss") sported a skull that was 9 feet (2.7 meters) long. To this day, no land animal has ever been found to have a larger sized skull!

Torosaurus

Which dinosaur had the largest teeth?

Funky Dino Fact 14:
Not surprising, this title goes to our fierce, well known friend, the *Tyrannosaurus rex*. Not only was it a very large and powerful meat-eater, but consider that fact that its teeth were more than 6 inches (15 centimeters) long.

Tyrannosaurus rex teeth

Which dinosaur had the longest neck?

Funky Dino Fact 15:
A plant-eating dinosaur found in parts of China called the *Mamenchisaurus* (say "Ma-men-chee-sore-uss") currently holds this record with a neck that was believe to measure roughly 36 feet (11 meters) in length. Scientist believe that they may one day discover a type of dinosaur with a neck length of up to 50 feet (15 meters) based on new partial dinosaur remains.

Mamenchisaurus

Which dinosaur had the largest set of claws?

Funky Dino Fact 16:
So far the "king of the claws" belongs to a Mongolian dinosaur from the late Cretaceous Period (75-70 million years ago) called *Therizinosaurus* (say "There-iz-in-owe-sore-uss"). Remains indicate that *Therizinosaurus* had arms 8 feet (2.4 meters) long with huge claws measuring 27.5 inches (72 centimeters) long. Originally classified as a meat-eating dinosaur, some scientists now believe that it may have actually eaten plants and insects such as termites and ants.

Thereizinosaurus

Which dinosaur had the biggest frill?

Funky Dino Fact 17:
A "frill" can be considered some type of body part sticking out from the main body of a dinosaur. One type of dinosaur called *Spinosaurus* (say "Spin-owe-sore-uss") sported a huge 5 foot (1.5 meter) mass of bony spikes that projected outwards from its backbone.

Spinosaurus

Which dinosaur had the longest crest?

Funky Dino Fact 18:
A "crest" can be thought of as something that sticks out from the head area of the dinosaur. Many types of dinosaurs had crests, however a type of "duck-billed" dinosaur called *Parasaurolophus* (say "Parah-sore-owe-loaf-uss") featured a very large hollow crest the projected backwards about 6 feet (1.8 meters) from its skull.

Parasaurolophus

Which dinosaur had the longest horns?

Funky Dino Fact 19:
Many of you will recognize the name of this dinosaur, the *Triceratops*. This dinosaur actually had 3 horns, one small horn on its nose and one longer horn over each eye. It is these eye horns that measured over 3 feet (0.9 meters) long that were unmatched in length by any other dinosaur species.

Triceratops

Which was the smallest of the dinosaurs?

Funky Dino Fact 20:
The award of the smallest of the dinosaurs currently goes to a tiny meat-eating dinosaur named *Compsognathus* (say "Comp-son-nay-thuss"). This little fellow is believed to have been only 4.5 feet (1.3 meters) long and weighed only 5-7 pounds (2-3 kilograms).

Compsognathus

How small was the smallest baby dinosaur ever found?

Funky Dino Fact 21:
Fossilized dinosaur eggs found in a nest of *Orodromeus* (say "Orrow-drom-ee-uss"), a plant-eating dinosaur, contained an embryo that measured only 4 inches (10 centimeters) long.

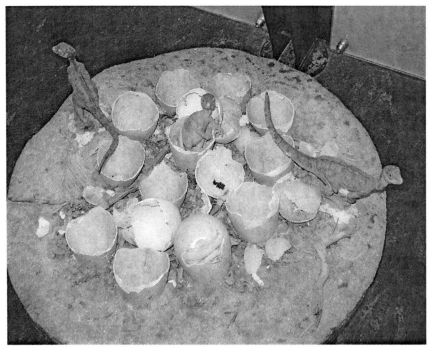

Orodromeus nest

Which dinosaur was the smartest?

Funky Dino Fact 22:

If we base our decision just on brain size, then the award of being the "smartest dinosaur" would belong to *Troodon* (say "Troe-owe-don"), a small meat-eating dinosaur found in parts of North America (Canada). The brain size of a *Troodon* would be about as big as some of today's birds.

Troodon

Which of the armoured dinosaurs was the smallest?

Funky Dino Fact 23:
An armoured dinosaur only discovered to have lived in parts of Eastern Europe, named *Struthiosaurus* (say "Strew-thee-oh-sore-uss"), holds the record as being the smallest of the armoured dinosaurs. *Struthiosaurus* is believed to have been only 6 feet (1.8 meters) long.

Struthiosaurus

Which dinosaur looked the most like a bird?

Funky Dino Fact 24:
Avimimus (say "Aye-vee-mim-uss"), a small meat-eating dinosaur roughly 5.5 feet (1.6 meters) long found in parts of Asia (Mongolia, China) is currently believed to be the dinosaur type that looked most like a bird based on its skeleton. Some scientists now believe that unlike most other dinosaurs that were covered with leathery skin, *Avimimus* may have been covered in feathers, however it probably was not able to fly, and ran on the ground like a modern day ostrich.

Avimimus

Which was the smallest of the horned dinosaurs?

Funky Dino Fact 25:
Found in Asia (China), a tiny horned dinosaur that was only about 30 inches (76 centimeters) long called *Microceratops* (say "My-croe-serra-tops") once lived. It had a tiny horn on its nose and a neck frill much like the larger versions.

Microceratops

Which was the smallest of the *tyrannosaur* species of dinosaurs?

Funky Dino Fact 26:
When we hear the word tyrannosaur, most of us think of the huge 40 foot (12 meters) long meat-eater, *Tyrannosaurus rex*, which was the terror of the prehistoric world when it lived many millions of years ago. You may be surprised to find out that the *tyrannosaur* species also had much smaller versions as well, with the smallest being the *Nanotyrannus* (say "Nah-no-tih-ran-uss"), that was only 15 feet (4.6 meters) long.

Nanotyrannus

Which dinosaur is believed to have had the biggest eyes?

Funky Dino Fact 27:
This "biggest eyes" award belongs to a dinosaur called *Dromiceiomimus* (say "Drom-ee-say-owe-mim-uss") that lived in parts of North America (Canada). This was another bird-like dinosaur and resembled a modern day ostrich without any feathers. With a pair of eyes believed to have measured 3 inches (7.5 centimeters) across, this dinosaur is believed to have had the biggest set of eyes.

Dromiceiomimus

Which dinosaur could run the fastest?

Funky Dino Fact 28:
Our new friend, *Dromiceiomimus*, may also hold the record as being the fastest dinosaur that ever lived. With its very long legs and bird-like frame, scientists believe that this dinosaur may have been able to exceed speeds of over 38 miles (60 kilometers) per hour.

Dromiceiomimus

Which dinosaur had the largest eggs ever found?

Funky Dino Fact 29:
Laying eggs that were 12 inches (30 centimeters) long and 10 inches (25 centimeters) in diameter, the *Ampelosaurus* (say "Am-pell-owe-sore-uss") currently holds the title as the layer of the largest dinosaur eggs.

Ampelosaurus

Which dinosaur group is thought to have lived the longest?

Funky Dino Fact 30:
If you are wondering as to which dinosaur group may have lived to be old folks according to their life span, then this title goes to a group of dinosaurs called sauropods, or what we most commonly call the long neck plant-eaters. A normal life span of one of these dinosaurs, if it could avoid being eaten or dying from sickness or disease, could reach as much as 100 years. So happy 100th birthday *Diplodocus* (say "Dip-lod-ick-uss")

Diplodocus

Which dinosaur had the tiniest brain?

Funky Dino Fact 31:
In humans, our brain size is calculated to be 1/50th of our body weight. The *Stegosaurus* had a brain size that was only 1/250,000 the weight of its body. Perhaps his nickname should be "pea-brain"?

Stegosaurus

Which dinosaurs had the biggest brains?

Funky Dino Fact 32:
The meat eating dinosaurs as a group are believed to have the largest brains in the dinosaur world, especially the smaller sized meat-eaters such as *Troodon*, which had a big brain in relation to its size. The brain of the dinosaurs did not focus on intelligence and thinking but rather skills needed for hunting and survival such as sight and hearing.

Troodon

Which of the plant-eating dinosaurs had the most teeth?

Funky Dino Fact 33:

A group of dinosaurs known as "duck-bills", which were two-footed plant-eaters, are thought to have the most teeth. For example *Corythosaurus* (say "Ko-rih-thoe-sore-uss") had several hundred teeth used for grinding tough plant material closely packed together in each of its jaws.

Corythosaurus

Which meat-eating dinosaur had the most teeth?

Funky Dino Fact 34:

If you guessed *Tyrannosaurus*, you would be wrong. The title of the meat-eater with the most teeth goes to a fish-eating dinosaur called *Baryonyx* (say "Bare-ee-on-icks"). With its long snout, *Baryonyx* had 32 teeth on each side of the its lower jaws which was twice as many as most other meat-eaters.

Baryonyx

What is the longest dinosaur name?

Funky Dino Fact 35:
How about this mouthful?
Micropachycephalosaurus (say "My-kro-pak-ee-sef-uh-lo-sore-uss"). Now with such a long name you might be expecting a huge dinosaur, but this dinosaur with the longest name happens to be one of the smallest plant-eating dinosaurs, being only about 20 inches long.

Micropachycephalosaurus

Where can you see the biggest mounted dinosaur skeleton?

Funky Dino Fact 36:
If you were to travel to the Humboldt Museum, located in Berlin, Germany, you could view a mounted skeleton of a *Brachiosaurus* that is over 72 feet (21.9 meters) long and it stands 19.5 feet (5.9 meters) high at the shoulder and the head is located 39 feet (11.8 meters) above the museum floor.

Brachiosaurus

Where can you see the tallest mounted dinosaur skeleton?

Funky Dino Fact 37:
The American Museum of Natural History located in New York City, in the United States, has on display a skeleton of long-necked plant-eater named *Barosaurus* (say "Bar-oh-sore-uss"). Standing on its hind legs, the head of the *Barosaurus* reaches 55 feet (16.7 meters) in the air measured from the museum floor.

Barosaurus

Which countries in the world have the most different types of dinosaur remains?

Funky Dino Fact 38:
At this time the United States tops of the list with 64 different types of dinosaurs being discovered, followed by Mongolia with 40 different types, China with 36 different types, Canada with 31 different types and the United Kingdom with 26 different types. As time goes on more dinosaur types will most certainly be discovered, so no one knows which country in the world will eventually top the list.

Map of the United States

How large was the biggest dinosaur bone ever discovered?

Funky Dino Fact 39:
In 1988, in the State of Colorado, United States, a hip structure of a long-necked plant-eater was discovered. This bone structure consisted of the hip bones with the backbones attached to it. It measured 6 feet (1.8 meters) high, 4.5 feet (1.4 meters) long and weighed close to 1,500 pounds (680 kilograms).

Large dinosaur bones

How long did the dinosaurs "rule the earth"?

Funky Dino Fact 40:
Most scientists agree that the dinosaurs ruled the Earth for over 160 million years, from the Triassic period around 230 million years ago through the Jurassic period and until the end of the Cretaceous period around 65 million years ago.

The Dinosaur Era   In Millions of Years before the Present

PALEOZOIC	MESOZOIC ERA			CENOZOIC
	TRIASSIC	JURASSIC	CRETACEOUS	PRESENT
300	250	200	150 100	50
First Reptiles	First Dinosaurs	Giant Dinosaurs First Birds	Zenith of the Dinosaurs Mass Extinction	Origin of Man

Dinosaur Timeline

Are dinosaurs classified as reptiles or birds?

Funky Dino Fact 41:
Get ready to be surprised! Recently scientists are thinking that dinosaurs may actually be related to birds and not reptiles as was once thought. In fact some new theories about dinosaurs are also suggesting that they may have been warm-blooded like us, rather than cold-blooded like reptiles such as snakes and lizards. So could the birds of today actually have evolved from the dinosaurs of yesterday?

Am I related to dinosaurs?

How fast could a large meat-eating dinosaur like *Tyrannosaurs rex* run?

Funky Dino Fact 42:
Best estimates as to how fast the large meat-eaters such as *Tyrannosaurus rex* could run have a top speed of between 10 to 30 miles per hour (20-50 km per hour).

Tyrannosaurus rex

What was the last dinosaur group to appear?

Funky Dino Fact 43:

A group of dinosaurs named "Ostrich dinosaurs" may have been one of the last types of dinosaurs to evolve before these magnificent creatures disappeared 65 million years ago. With beaks and long necks similar to a modern Ostrich, these dinosaurs also looked much different having long tails and long arms with claws for digging and were covered in skin, not feathers. They depended on their speed rather than size and strength to survive. One example is *Ornithomimus* (say "Or-nith-owe-mim-uss") which lived in the western parts of the United States and stood over 2 meters (6.5 feet) tall. These dinosaurs were known as omnivores, meaning they ate both meat and plants.

Ornithomimus

Did any dinosaurs have two brains?

Funky Dino Fact 44:
No! At one time some scientists believed that some of very large plant-eating dinosaurs such as *Apatosaurus* (say "Ap-at-owe-sore-uss") may have need two brains due to their huge body size. Research has shown this idea of some dinosaurs having 2 brains to be totally false.

Apatosaurus

Did any dinosaurs have feathers?

Funky Dino Fact 45:
Recent scientific research has found more than 30 kinds of dinosaurs may have had feathers based on feather fossils found in China. This makes sense if you believe the most recent theories that are now linking birds as living descendants of dinosaurs. This does not mean that dinosaurs could fly or had wings, but rather feathers may have been used to keep warm, attract mates or as a way of hiding. Perhaps the most famous of the dinosaurs with feathers is *Archaeopteryx* (say "Ark-ee-op-tur-icks") currently believed to be the earliest known link to modern birds.

Archaeopteryx

Could dinosaurs swim?

Funky Dino Fact 46:
Until recently scientist were not sure if dinosaurs could actually swim rather than just wade into the water. New evidence now shows that most dinosaurs, even the large meat-eaters like *Allosaurus* (say "Al-owe-sore-uss") were capable of swimming at least for short distances in much the same way that modern animals such as bears are able to swim.

Allosaurus

What was the name of first dinosaur discovered?

Funky Dino Fact 47:
The first dinosaur to be discovered was found in England in 1824 and given the name *Megalosaurus* (say "Meg-ah-low-sore-uss").

Megalosaurus

Were dinosaurs social animals?

Funky Dino Fact 48:
Yes, some kinds of dinosaurs lived in groups and travelled or migrated together in herds just like modern day animals such as caribou. Some dinosaurs such as the *Hadrosaurus* (say "Had-roe-sore-uss") even had nesting grounds which were returned to year after year where eggs were laid and the young were born and taken care of.

Hadrosaurus

Could dinosaur talk to each other?

Funky Dino Fact 49:
Just like animals we see today, there is no reason to think that dinosaurs did not communicate both visually by head shaking, foot stomping, etc. and vocally through grunts, roars and bellowing. Dinosaurs such as the *Torosaurus* (say "Torr-owe-sore-uss") had a large frill that may have changed in appearance when the animal was threatened.

Torosaurus

Why did some dinosaurs grow so big?

Funky Dino Fact 50:
Scientist believe that the huge size of some of the plant-eating dinosaurs known as sauropods was largely due to their food supply. These dinosaurs, such as *Supersaurus* (say "Soo-pur-sore-uss"), found most of their food in the tops of trees and the types of leaves and needles they ate were very tough meaning they needed to have huge stomachs to digest this type of food. Their huge size also protected them from many smaller meat-eaters plus it helped to insulate their bodies against overheating in the hot sun and to avoid heat loss at night.

Supersaurus

Were most dinosaurs meat-eaters or plant-eaters?

Funky Dino Fact 51:
There were far more kinds of plant-eating dinosaurs than meat-eating dinosaurs. The reason for this is because in any level of a food chain there must be more producers of food than consumers of food. So in the case of dinosaurs, there were more plants than plant-eaters which ate the plants, and then in turn there were more plant-eaters than there were meat-eaters who ate the plant-eaters.

Tyrannosaurus verses Triceratops

Did any mammals live during the time of the dinosaurs?

Funky Dino Fact 52:
Many people believe that mammals group (to which all humans belong to) arrived on earth only after the dinosaurs had been long gone. Actually there were mammals during dinosaur times, however early mammals were very small compared to the dinosaurs, such as the *Megazostrodon* (say "Meg-ah-zos-troe-don") which was only 10-12 centimeters (4-5 inches) long, and weighed only 50 grams (2 ounces) making it not much larger than a mouse. To avoid being eaten by all the larger dinosaurs, it probably only came out at night to eat insects, grubs and worms.

Megazostrodon

Could any dinosaurs fly?

Funky Dino Fact 53:

No, there were no flying dinosaurs. The large creatures you often see flying around in books and movies about dinosaurs such as *Pteranodon* (say "Tear-ann-owe-don"), were called pterosaurs, and are not classified as dinosaurs but rather winged reptiles.

Pteranodon

Did any dinosaurs live in the oceans and seas?

Funky Dino Fact 54:
No, once again by definition, dinosaurs had to be land animals. So while there were huge creatures living in the oceans and seas during the time of the dinosaurs, such as the massive *Liopleurodon* (say "Lie-owe-plure-owe-don"), which may have reached the size of 49-66 feet (15-20 meters) and weighed as much as 50 tons, it was not a dinosaur.

Liopleurodon

Which dinosaur is known as "King of the Dinosaurs"?

Funky Dino Fact 55:

For nearly 90 years, the *Tyrannosaurs rex*, held the crown as "King of the Dinosaurs" and is perhaps the most well known of all dinosaurs. Then in 1994, in the country of Argentina (South America) a skeleton of an even larger meat-eater was found. Later named *Giganotosaurus* (say "Jee-gah-noe-toe-sore-uss") this beast is believed to be 3-6 feet (1-2 meters) bigger and 2000 pounds (1 ton) heavier than *Tyrannosaurus rex*. So for now, *Giganotosaurus* is the reigning "King of the Dinosaurs".

Giganotosaurus

I hope you enjoyed this book! Here are some of my other dinosaur book titles you may also be interested in (currently available from the Amazon Kindle book store).

Dinosaur Books For Kids: The Menacing Meat-Eaters
Dinosaur Books For Kids: The Peaceful Plant-Eaters
Dinosaur Books For Kids: Dinosaur Alphabet Soup

* You can also find more information about dinosaurs and easy links to these other books at my Dino Detective website:
http://www.thedinodetective.com/

Now that you have finished reading this book, could you please leave a book review at the Amazon book store to let me know if you liked the book or not. Thank you!

Sincerely,

THE DINO DETECTIVE

Dinosaur Images and Photograph Credits

Herrerasaurus image by Tom Duca on Flickr, used under the Creative Commons Attribution license

Staurikosaurus image by Nobu Tamara on Wikimedia Commons, used under the Creative Commons Attribution license

Asteroid image by State Farm on Flickr, used under the Creative Commons Attribution license

Tyrannosaurus image by Lehigh Valley PA on Flickr, used under the Creative Commons license

Image purchased from Canstock Photo License #2326836

Allosarus image by Sporst on Flickr, used under the Creative Commons license

Brachiosaurus image by Mystic Country CT on Flickr, used under the Creative Commons Attribution license

Stegosaurus image by Kim Scarborough on Flickr, used under the Creative Commons Attribution license

Triceratops image by milpool79 on Flickr, used under the Creative Commons Attribution license

Iguanodon image by mhaller1979 on Flickr, used under the Creative Commons Attribution license

Psittacosaurus image by cliff1066 on Flickr, used under the Creative Commons Attribution license

Minmi image by London looks on Flickr, used under the Creative Commons Attribution license

Alaska dinosaur footprint image courtesy of Roland Gangloff, University of Alaska Museum

Ultrasauros image by cliff1066 on Flickr, used under the Creative Commons Attribution licens

Ultasauros image by LeCire on Public Domain, used under the Creative Commons Attribution license

Seismosaurus image on Public Domain, used under the Creative Commons Attribution license

Ankylosaurus image by britl on Flickr, used under the Creative Commons Attribution license

CPSIA information can be obtained
at www.ICGtesting.com
Printed in the USA
LVOW07s1500231017

553448LV00041B/1815/P